The Best Christmas Pageant Ever Movie Review

A Comprehensive Guide to Laughter, Love, and Life Lessons for the Holiday Season

Stacey J. Tengan

Packed with exclusive production notes, fun facts, interactive quizzes, and thought-provoking discussion questions!

Gratitude!

Dear Reader,

Thank you for reading my movie review of **The Best Christmas Pageant Ever Movie Review**, I appreciate your time and attention. I enjoyed writing this movie review, and I hope you learned from it.

Please leave a review or rating for my book and share it with others.

Please check out my other books and visit my website. Thank you for your support. I appreciate you!

All rights reserved. No part of this publication may be reproduced, distributed, or transmitted in any form or by any means, including photocopying, recording, or other electronic or mechanical methods, without the prior written permission of the publisher, except in the case of brief quotations embodied in critical reviews and certain other noncommercial uses permitted by copyright law.

Copyright ©Stacey J. Tengan, 2024.

DISCLAIMER

This book is for educational and informational purposes only, reflecting the author's personal opinions and interpretations of the movie **"The Best Christmas Pageant Ever Movie Review"**.

The author does not claim ownership of the movie or any related intellectual property, and all references are used under fair use for critique and analysis. The author has made every effort to ensure the accuracy of the information presented in this book. The author does not intend to cause harm or infringe on any rights. This work aims to provide insights and foster discussion about the movie **"The Best Christmas Pageant Ever Movie Review"**

Table Of Content

Chapter 1: Introduction

Chapter 2: Plot Summary

Chapter 3: Character Analysis

Chapter 4: Themes and Messages

Chapter 5 - Direction and Cinematography

Chapter 6: Performances

Chapter 7: Comparison with the Book

Chapter 8: Audience Reception

Chapter 9: Conclusion

Chapter 10: Additional Resources

ABOUT THE AUTHOR

Exclusive Christmas Preview

Chapter 1: Introduction

Exclusive Production Notes

- **Initial Conception:** The idea for the film adaptation of *"The Best Christmas Pageant Ever"* began with director Dallas Jenkins, who was deeply inspired by Barbara Robinson's book. Jenkins envisioned bringing the chaotic yet heartwarming story to life with a blend of humor and emotion.

- **Casting Choices:** Judy Greer was cast as Grace Bradley for her ability to balance comedic timing with heartfelt moments. The casting of the Herdman siblings was a meticulous process, seeking children who could portray both mischief and vulnerability.

Overview of "The Best Christmas Pageant Ever"

The excellent Dallas Jenkins directs "The Best Christmas Pageant Ever," a vivid and engaging version of Barbara Robinson's beloved children's book that captures the soul of the holiday season. This wonderful film, released on November 8, 2024, stars the ever-charming Judy Greer, the talented Lauren Graham, and the humorously endearing Pete Holmes.

The Herdmans, a famed group of six siblings known for their crazy antics and disruptive conduct, are central to this story. They are the type of children who appear to live in disorder, frequently causing havoc wherever they go. When these rambunctious children unexpectedly take over the local church's traditional Christmas pageant, the neighborhood braces for a riot of hilarity and chaos.

However, what follows is more than just a sequence of humorous misadventures; it is a serious examination of what Christmas truly means. Amidst the chaos and humor, the Herdmans make a heartfelt realization about love, acceptance, and the spirit of giving that resonates strongly with the audience.

This adaption expertly mixes humor and heartfelt moments, reminding us that even in the most chaotic situations, there is still room for growth and understanding. The film asks audiences to consider their own holiday experiences—how we are frequently caught up in traditions and expectations, only to learn that the actual magic is found in connection and compassion.

Personal Connection to the Story

As someone who has spent 5 years working in journalism, I have seen innumerable stories that have moved me. However, none have struck a deeper chord with me than "The Best Christmas Pageant Ever." Watching this film was like stepping into a time machine, transporting me back to my own childhood—a period of innocence, joy, and communal spirit. Growing up in a small town, I took part in community plays and pageants that brought neighbors together to celebrate. The camaraderie among friends, the excitement in the air as we prepared our lines, and even the occasional blunder that turned into an internal joke are all memories I treasure.

This film is more than simply a charming story; it's a sad reminder of the little joys that fill our hearts with memories. Moments when we gather together as a community to celebrate our common traditions are priceless. They remind us of our interconnectedness and the comfort that comes with belonging.

When I first watched "The Best Christmas Pageant Ever," I was struck by how well it depicted the Herdmans' metamorphosis. Their journey is one of redemption, a poignant story about seeing beyond superficial prejudices and accepting people's innate goodness. It's easy to disregard those who appear unusual or difficult; nevertheless, this narrative reminds us to look past appearances and discover the potential for kindness and love in everyone.

The film's themes are especially relevant during the Christmas season, when we frequently reflect on our ideals of kindness, forgiveness, and unity. It pushes us to open our hearts to those who do not conform to our preconceived conceptions of "normal."

The Herdmans teach us that everyone deserves a second opportunity, and that genuine acceptance can result in unexpected friendships.

In a society filled with division and misunderstanding, "The Best Christmas Pageant Ever" is a gentle reminder that we are all human, flawed yet capable of improvement. It encourages us to accept our differences while finding common ground in our shared humanity. As we gather with loved ones this holiday season, let us carry on the attitude of acceptance that this film so beautifully captures. It's not only about enjoying Christmas; it's about celebrating each other—our differences, our stories, and our ability to love.

Fun Facts

- **Book to Screen:** Barbara Robinson's book has been a staple in school curriculums and community theaters for decades before being adapted into a film.

- **On-Set Antics:** The young actors playing the Herdman siblings often improvised their lines, adding to the authenticity of their unruly behavior.

-**Holiday Release:** The film was strategically released in early November to kick off the holiday movie season.

Interactive Quiz

1. Who is the director of *"The Best Christmas Pageant Ever"*?
   - a) Dallas Jenkins
   - b) Steven Spielberg

- c) Christopher Nolan
- d) Tim Burton

2. What is the name of the character played by Judy Greer?
   - a) Beth Bradley
   - b) Grace Bradley
   - c) Imogene Herdman
   - d) Mrs. Armstrong

3. When was *"The Best Christmas Pageant Ever"* released in theaters?
   - a) December 25, 2023
   - b) November 8, 2024
   - c) January 1, 2025
   - d) October 31, 2024

Discussion Questions

- Why do you think the story of *"The Best Christmas Pageant Ever"* continues to resonate with audiences of all ages?

- How does the movie's depiction of the Herdmans challenge traditional notions of what makes a "good" or "bad" person?

- Reflect on a personal experience where you saw someone change for the better. How does this relate to the Herdmans' transformation in the movie?

Chapter 2: Plot Summary

Exclusive Production Notes

- *Faithful Adaptation:* The screenplay aimed to stay as faithful as possible to the original book, with many of the dialogues taken directly from Barbara Robinson's text.

- *Community Involvement:* The movie's production involved local community members as extras in the church and pageant scenes, adding authenticity to the setting.

Introduction to the Herdmans

Consider the most disruptive and unruly children you can think of. Now multiply that mayhem by six, and you have the Herdmans. This legendary group of siblings—Imogene, Ralph, Leroy, Claude, Ollie, and Gladys—are the pinnacle of mischief and mayhem in their little town. These youngsters are well-known for their bizarre conduct, which includes lying, stealing, cursing, and bullying their friends with reckless abandon, sending shivers down their parents' spines. They live in a crumbling house that looks to droop from neglect, with an absentee mother who seems more concerned with her own life than her children's well-being. Other parents tell their children to avoid the Herdmans—"Stay away from them!"—and for good cause. Their reputation as troublemakers is well-deserved, yet it is precisely their unpredictable nature that sets the stage for their unexpected involvement in the Christmas pageant. This surprise transforms their wild energy into something wonderfully endearing.

The Challenge of directing the pageant

Enter Grace Bradley, portrayed by the brilliant Judy Greer. Grace is a well-intentioned but overburdened lady who is unwillingly assigned to conduct the annual Christmas pageant after Mrs. Armstrong, the usual director, fractures her leg in a fall. Grace is first thrilled with delight and a desire to start a lovely Christmas tradition for her town, but her optimism fades when she hears who attended tryouts. The Herdmans come not because they are in the Christmas mood, but because the possibility of free sweets is an appealing draw for these youngsters, who regularly go hungry.

As tryouts begin, it's clear that the Herdmans have no idea what a Christmas pageant is. They embrace key roles with abandon: Imogene plays Mary with a rebellious attitude; Ralph plays Joseph as if it were just another opportunity to cause trouble; Gladys insists on becoming the Lord's Angel; and Leroy, Claude, and Ollie round out the group as the wise men. What follows is a series of funny mishaps and misunderstandings that will have viewers laughing and groaning. The Herdmans' ignorance of the Christmas story results in bizarre interpretations; for example, Imogene insists on smoking a cigar while portraying Mary, a terrifying sight that leaves Grace speechless, and Gladys prefers to shout her lines rather than repeat them gently.

Despite the chaos, Grace is determined to stage a successful pageant. Her journey becomes one of patience and endurance as she navigates the tumultuous waters generated by these unruly kids. Each practice feels like an uphill fight against not just their pranks, but also her doubts about her capacity to carry out this pageant.

Key Moments in the Story

The narrative takes a melancholy turn as the Herdmans learn the true meaning of Christmas. As they read of Jesus' birth—the humble beginnings of a child born in a barn without even a decent crib—they begin to understand Mary's circumstances. Imogene is particularly moved by this thought, and she begins to relate with Mary as a little girl facing huge challenges. This increased understanding softens their hard edges and begins a metamorphosis within them.

Grace notices an unexpected moment during rehearsal: Imogene silently reflects on what it means to be Mary, a young mother struggling with fear and uncertainty. This moment of vulnerability is surprising because it reveals that underneath their hard exteriors lies a want for connection and understanding. The other Herdmans start to show signs of change as well, asking questions about the narrative and becoming interested in its deeper meanings.

When pageant night approaches, there is an undeniable sense of anticipation. The entire town clutches its breath, waiting for what everyone expects would be a disastrous performance filled with blunders and chaos. However, what follows is nothing short of incredible. The Herdmans portray the nativity story with real honesty, captivating everyone in attendance. Imogene's tear-stained face as she cradles a baby doll of Jesus strikes a connection with the spectator; it represents both innocence and power.

Gladys' enthusiastic shout, "Hey!" "Unto you, a child is born!" echoes through the church, moving hearts. The townspeople are startled by how deeply these misfit youngsters relate to a narrative they previously knew little about. As chaos erupts around them, their rough delivery and spontaneous moments create an environment drenched with genuine emotion, and the performance transforms into something profound: a visceral portrait of hope and love that embodies the true spirit of Christmas.

The finale provides an important lesson:

Despite their flaws and chaotic temperament, the Herdmans have breathed new life into a traditional narrative. Their genuine approach removes any pretense associated with holiday performances, focusing on what is essential during this season—compassion for one another and love for those who are sometimes overlooked or viciously attacked.

Their transformation from troublemakers to surprising heroes serves as a reminder that Christmas is about recognizing our common humanity and finding joy in unexpected places, rather than perfection or polished presentations. In this way, "The Best Christmas Pageant Ever" becomes more than simply a narrative about children putting on a show; it is also a celebration of atonement, acceptance, and the transformative power of love during one of the happiest times of the year.

Fun Facts

- ***Real-Life Inspiration:*** Barbara Robinson based the characters of the Herdmans on children she knew growing up, lending a sense of realism to their antics.

- ***Behind-the-Scenes:*** During filming, the young actors portraying the Herdmans formed a tight-knit group, much like their characters.

Interactive Quiz

1. What motivates the Herdmans to audition for the Christmas pageant?
   - a) A dare from their friends
   - b) A desire to cause trouble
   - c) The promise of free snacks
   - d) Their love for acting

2. Who plays the role of Joseph in the pageant?
   - a) Claude Herdman
   - b) Ralph Herdman
   - c) Leroy Herdman
   - d) Ollie Herdman

3. What is the turning point for the Herdmans' understanding of the Christmas story?
   - a) When they rehearse their lines
   - b) When they see the nativity scene
   - c) When they hear about the birth of Jesus
   - d) When they are given their costumes

Discussion Questions

- Discuss how the Herdmans' lack of knowledge about the Christmas story impacts their interpretation of the pageant. What does this say about their upbringing and environment?

- How does Grace Bradley handle the challenges of directing the pageant? What qualities make her an effective leader in this situation?

- What key moments in the story signify the Herdmans' transformation? How do these moments affect the other characters in the movie?

Chapter 3: Character Analysis

Exclusive Production Notes:

- ***Character Depth:*** Dallas Jenkins focused on adding depth to the characters, particularly the Herdmans, to ensure their transformation felt genuine and impactful.

- ***Actor Preparations:*** Judy Greer and Beatrice Schneider (Imogene Herdman) spent time together off set to build a believable rapport, enhancing their on-screen interactions.

Grace Bradley (Judy Greer)

Grace Bradley, played by the talented Judy Greer, emerges as the unsung hero of "The Best Christmas Pageant Ever." When the regular director, Mrs. Armstrong, breaks her leg, Grace is thrust into the role of director for the annual Christmas pageant. Grace embodies a blend of patience, resilience, and an unwaveringly kind-hearted personality. Her transformation from a reluctant volunteer to a motivated leader is both uplifting and realistic, highlighting the difficulties many people confront when venturing outside of their comfort zones.

Grace is overwhelmed with a combination of excitement and dread about competing in the pageant from the start of the film. She envisions a traditional Christmas event that would bring joy to her town.

However, her excitement rapidly fades as she discovers she must handle not just the event's logistics but also the unpredictable pandemonium brought on by the Herdman twins. As she deals with their crazy antics—ranging from Imogene's bold disobedience to Ralph's roughness—Grace finds herself balancing her roles as a mother, community member, and now director.

What distinguishes Grace is her ability to recognize opportunities where others see problems. Instead of rejecting the Herdmans as troublemakers, she chooses to interact with them, realizing that underneath their disruptive conduct is a need for acceptance and connection.

This ability to empathize enables her to build a relationship with the Herdmans, particularly Imogene, as she learns to negotiate their intricacies. Grace's character acts as a critical link between these quirky youngsters and the doubting villagers, proving that empathy and understanding can overcome even the most formidable obstacles.

Grace's drive is evident throughout the film, particularly in moments of weakness and strength. She endures countless difficulties, including chaotic rehearsals, community distrust, and her own misgivings, but each one strengthens her drive. Her journey from insecurity to confidence is brilliantly shown, as she learns to appreciate imperfection and discover beauty in unexpected places. Finally, Grace epitomizes the Christmas spirit of nurturing love and acceptance, which may improve people's lives.

Imogene Herdman(Beatrice Schneider)

Imogene Herdman, played beautifully by Beatrice Schneider, stands out as the eldest and most fearsome of the Herdman siblings. Imogene, who is first viewed as the ringleader of their mischievous adventures, experiences a profound shift after learning about the Christmas tale. Schneider nails

Imogene's rawness and tenderness underneath her rough exterior, resulting in a nuanced and engaging character.

Imogene appears to be the epitome of disobedience; she is loud, boisterous, and unrepentant about her identity. However, when she takes on the part of Mary during pageant preparations, we see a significant difference in her manner. The more she hears about Mary's struggles—a young girl giving birth in a barn with little comfort or support—the more she recognizes her own sentiments of rejection and sorrow. Schneider's portrayal eloquently conveys this awakening; we witness Imogene fight with her background while taking on a role that needs emotional depth.

Imogene's turning moment occurs during a rehearsal when she experiences a realization about Mary's condition. She realizes that Mary was more than simply a character in a novel; she experienced genuine obstacles such as fear of judgment, anxiety about parenthood, and solitude. This insight softens Imogene's harsh edges and enables her to display vulnerability for the first time. As she depicts Mary with such real emotion—tears running down her cheeks while clutching a baby doll representing Jesus—she affects not just herself but also how others see her.

Imogene's transition from resistance to empathy is crucial to the film's message of redemption and understanding. By accepting her job with sincerity rather than sarcasm or disobedience, she eventually helps to heal divisions in her society and demonstrates that everyone has something meaningful to contribute.

Beth Bradley (Molly Bell Wright)

Beth Bradley, performed by the excellent Molly Belle Wright, is both the narrator and one of the primary characters in this moving drama. Beth, Grace Bradley's daughter, offers a fresh viewpoint on the events developing inside their church group. Initially dubious of the Herdmans' participation in the pageant, regarding them as nothing more than troublemakers, Beth's perspective eventually evolves to one of adoration as she observes their surprising metamorphosis.

Wright's performance conveys Beth's innocence while simultaneously emphasizing her developing understanding of human complexity. Throughout the film, we witness Beth manage her own sentiments about friendship and acceptance; she struggles with societal standards while longing for honesty in relationships. Beth learns essential lessons about compassion and understanding as she interacts with Imogene and sees past her harsh demeanor, learning that everyone has their own challenges.

One especially moving scene happens when Beth observes Imogene during practice; rather than being scared by her presence or dismissing her as simply another troublemaker, Beth begins to empathize with Imogene's hardships. This scene signifies Beth's transformation from childlike innocence to a greater awareness of human nature, a motif that runs throughout the film.

Beth's transformation acts as a mirror for viewers, reminding us that genuine understanding frequently comes from putting aside preconceived assumptions and welcoming each other's tales with open hearts. Her character represents hope for future generations, demonstrating that change is possible when we choose compassion over judgment.

Other Main Characters

Ralph Herdman (Jaxon Ashworth):
Ralph is presented as the eldest Herdman boy who competes against Joseph in the pageant. Initially gruff around the edges, like his siblings, Ralph's temperament softens when he realizes the significance of his position. His voyage shows unexpected depths; he learns responsibility while struggling with his identity amid his turbulent family dynamic.

Gladys Herdman (Emma Jacobson):
Gladys is described as the youngest and most energetic of the Herdmans; she tackles her part as the Angel of the Lord with boundless zeal, adding both comedy and heart to every scene she appears in. Her

loud proclamations are frequently received with amusement, but they also demonstrate how real joy can encourage others around us.

- **Mrs. Armstrong (Lauren Graham):** As the original pageant director who was hampered by injury, Mrs. Armstrong provides comedic relief while also embodying some of the town's initial opposition to change. Lauren Graham's acting maintains a good mix of wit and tenderness; as Mrs. Armstrong's character arc progresses from skepticism to discovery of potential, viewers see how even individuals who are first skeptical may find delight in unexpected circumstances.

Each character in "The Best Christmas

Pageant Ever" adds their own flavor to this diverse tapestry of personalities and experiences. We witness a wonderful message emerge from their encounters, which are full of humor, conflict, development, and redemption: everyone, regardless of background or previous misdeeds, has the possibility for good transformation.

In this sense, "The Best Christmas Pageant Ever" becomes more than just a holiday story; it is an investigation of change through compassion—a reminder that love knows no bounds and that genuine connection may arise from the most unlikely places. The characters' travels are not only entertaining but also meaningful reflections on our own lives during this season of giving—a plea to accept our common humanity and find joy despite our differences.

Fun Facts

- *Method Acting:* The actors playing the Herdman siblings stayed in character between takes to maintain their unruly energy.
- *Improvisation:* Many of the Herdmans' lines were ad-libbed by the young actors, adding authenticity to their performances.

Interactive Quiz

1. Which character serves as the narrator of the story?
- a) Grace Bradley

- b) Imogene Herdman
- c) Beth Bradley
- d) Mrs. Armstrong

2. How is Imogene Herdman portrayed at the beginning of the movie?
   - a) Shy and reserved
   - b) Tough and rebellious
   - c) Cheerful and optimistic
   - d) Quiet and studious

3. What role does Lauren Graham's character play in the community?
   - a) The school principal
   - b) The church choir director
   - c) The original pageant director
   - d) The mayor

Discussion Questions

- Analyze the character of Grace Bradley. How does her role as the pageant director change her perception of the Herdmans?
- Discuss the character development of Imogene Herdman. What aspects of her personality make her a compelling character?

- How do the interactions between Beth Bradley and the Herdmans highlight the themes of understanding and acceptance?

Chapter 4: Themes and Messages

Exclusive Production Notes:

- ***Theme Development:*** The film places a strong emphasis on themes of redemption and community, aiming to highlight the importance of second chances and acceptance.

- ***Holiday Spirit:*** The production team worked to infuse every scene with the holiday spirit, from set design to music, enhancing the film's festive atmosphere.

The True Meaning of Christmas

At its core, "The Best Christmas Pageant Ever" is a moving exploration of the true meaning of Christmas. The Herdmans, known for their wild and disruptive behavior, begin the story with a limited understanding of what the holiday truly means. To them, Christmas is just another opportunity to wreak havoc and enjoy the thrill of violating social norms. However, as they join in the church's Christmas pageant, they and the audience go on a transformative journey that demonstrates that Christmas is more than simply music, bright lights, and presents wrapped in glossy paper. Ultimately, everything comes down to compassion, forgiveness, and the transformational power of unconditional love.

As the Herdmans dive into the nativity story, their candid and genuine thoughts challenge the community's preconceived notions about what it means to celebrate Christmas. For example, Imogene's representation of Mary evolves from an act of disobedience to a true picture of a young mother confronted with huge challenges. Initially, she accepts the role with confidence, smoking a cigar to show her opposition. However, when Imogene learns more about Mary's struggles—giving birth in a stable and surviving societal judgment—she begins to portray the character with genuine emotion. This transformation proves that everyone, regardless of background or prior behavior, can grasp and communicate the true spirit of Christmas.

The film encourages viewers to rethink their interpretations of the holiday and embrace its more profound meanings beyond commercialism. It prompts us to consider how we might cultivate kindness in our interactions and practice forgiveness in our relationships. The emotional weight of this message reverberates throughout the film, reminding us that love can conquer difficulties and that everyone has the potential to change if given the opportunity. In this regard, "The Best Christmas Pageant Ever" serves as a poignant reminder that Christmas is more than just a day on the calendar—it's an opportunity to open our hearts to others.

Redemption & Second Chances

Redemption is a significant theme throughout the film. The Herdmans are first seen as hopeless troublemakers, with a reputation that accompanies them—"the worst kids in the world." This label instills distrust among the people, who believe these children are beyond correction or comprehension. However, as the narrative unfolds, we begin to see them in a new light. Their involvement in the Christmas pageant provides a unique opportunity for transformation, not just for themselves, but also for others around them.

The Herdmans' journey from outcasts to

prominent characters in the pageant sends a compelling message: everyone deserves another chance. As they accept their responsibilities and learn about the essence of Christmas, they reveal both their weaknesses and their virtues. This theme resonates powerfully during the Christmas season, which is often associated with new beginnings and hopes for a brighter future. Finally, the film implies that everyone willing to embrace change and open oneself up to love and acceptance may discover redemption.

Imogene's character growth is particularly poignant; her journey from defiance to empathy exemplifies this idea. Through her portrayal of Mary, she learns not just about love but also about her worth. This journey emphasizes that no one is beyond redemption and that an unexpected encounter, such as participating in a Christmas pageant, can spark profound change inside us.

The video also depicts how communal perceptions may shift when people are allowed the freedom to express themselves truthfully. As the townspeople witness Imogene's emotional performance on stage, they identify her as more than just a troublemaker, but as someone capable of deep feelings and empathy. This shift in perspective provides an environment conducive to healing, not only for the Herdmans but for everyone involved.

Community and Family Values

"*The Best Christmas Pageant Ever*" highlights the importance of community and family values. Initially, local church members are hesitant to welcome the Herdmans into their midst, viewing them with suspicion and scorn due to their legendary status. However, as they collaborate to prepare for the pageant, barriers begin to crumble, resulting in true friendships amongst people from all backgrounds.

Grace Bradley's role as pageant director is crucial in strengthening these bonds. Her tolerance and sensitivity help to close the gap between the Herdmans and the rest of the community. Grace demonstrates that understanding may flourish when compassion takes precedence over judgment. This technique illustrates how accepting diversity may improve community connections and promote collective growth.

As rehearsals progress, we see how Grace's leadership inspires others to overcome their preconceptions. The villagers eventually understand the Herdmans' humanity; they no longer see them as troublemakers but as individuals worthy of respect and acceptance. This shift in perspective provides an environment conducive to healing, not only for the Herdmans but for everyone involved.

The Herdmans experience a new sense of family via their involvement in the pageant. Despite their chaotic home life, which is characterized by neglect and absence, they begin to experience a feeling of belonging in this loving community. As they engage with others during rehearsals, they discover acceptance, which softens their hard edges and allows them to open out emotionally in ways they never had before.

This sense of belonging enriches not just their individual lives, but also the entire community. The video masterfully portrays how shared experiences can foster bonds that cross boundaries, reminding us that we are stronger together.

In conclusion, *"The Best Christmas Pageant Ever"* is more than a delightful holiday film; it brilliantly ties together themes of discovering the true meaning of Christmas, atonement, and the power of community and family values. The film's depiction of the Herdmans' journey from outcasts to beloved participants serves as a powerful reminder that everyone is capable of change.

As viewers consider these themes in their own lives, they are asked to consider how they might apply these values beyond December 25th. The film urges us to approach each day with an open heart, knowing that even the most unexpected individuals may teach us great lessons about love and acceptance.

Finally, *"The Best Christmas Pageant Ever"* conveys a positive message: regardless of our past or present circumstances, we all have the power to grow and connect through compassion—the real spirit of Christmas that can brighten even the darkest of conditions. This film not only entertains, but also inspires us to be better versions of ourselves—to reach out with empathy to those who are hurting or misunderstood—and to remember that together, we can create a community filled with warmth, compassion, and love at this beautiful time of year.

In short, "The Best Christmas Pageant Ever" challenges us all to incorporate its ideals into our daily lives: choosing compassion over judgment, seeking understanding over conflict, and accepting that everyone has a story worth telling—a lesson that will last far after the holiday season.

Fun Facts

- **Community Spirit:** Many of the extras in the pageant scenes were residents, bringing a genuine sense of community to the film.

- **Holiday Traditions:** The cast and crew shared their favorite holiday traditions during filming, fostering a festive environment on set.

Interactive Quiz

1. What is one of the central themes of the movie?

- a) The importance of wealth
- b) The power of kindness and redemption
- c) The value of competition
- d) The joy of material gifts

2. How do the Herdmans' actions change the community's perception of them?

- a) They become more feared
- b) They are ignored
- c) They are embraced and accepted
- d) They are punished

3. What does the movie suggest about the true meaning of Christmas?

- a) It is about giving and receiving gifts
- b) It is about community, love, and redemption

- c) It is about attending church services
- d) It is about having the perfect holiday celebration

Discussion Questions

- Reflect on the theme of redemption in the movie. How do the Herdmans exemplify this theme?

- Discuss the significance of the community coming together to support the pageant. What does this reveal about the power of collective effort?

- How does the movie redefine traditional notions of the Christmas spirit? What lessons can viewers take away from the Herdmans' journey?

Chapter 5 - Direction and Cinematography

Exclusive Production Notes

- Visual Storytelling: Dallas Jenkins used a combination of wide shots and close-ups to capture the chaos and emotion of the pageant, creating a visually engaging experience.

-Lighting and Atmosphere: Natural lighting and warm tones were used to create a cozy, festive atmosphere, enhancing the holiday spirit.

Dallas Jenkins' approach

Dallas Jenkins, a director known for his ability to combine humor and heartfelt storytelling, brings a unique and refreshing perspective to "The Best Christmas Pageant Ever." His approach is distinguished by a careful balance of comedic elements and emotional depth, ensuring that the film appeals to audiences of all ages. Jenkins recognizes that this narrative is about more than simply the Herdman brothers' pranks; it's about the transformational power of Christmas and the lessons we learn along the way.

Jenkins outlines a clear objective for the picture from a distance: to transcend a simple, comic story into a moving meditation of human connection and redemption. He does this by emphasizing character development and realistic storytelling, allowing the viewer to form strong bonds with both the Herdmans and the other characters in the movie. Each character is allowed the opportunity to develop, making their stories more relevant and poignant.

Jenkins' directing elevates what could have been a simple children's story to a complex, multilayered drama brimming with authentic emotion. He expertly balances amusing moments with more meaningful themes, reminding audiences that even in the middle of turmoil and mischief, there is still potential for development, understanding, and love. His ability to get genuine performances from his ensemble allows for vulnerable moments that connect with spectators. The Herdmans' metamorphosis from reputed troublemakers to respected community members is a striking reminder that everyone can change.

Furthermore, Jenkins uses a variety of cinematic methods to improve storytelling. He masters timing, enabling humorous moments to breathe while simultaneously heightening suspense in dramatic passages. This pace keeps viewers interested and involved in the characters' travels. His attention to detail in directing actors, which encourages them to connect with their characters' emotions, leads to performances that are authentic and empathetic.

Visual Style and Setting

The visual style of "The Best Christmas Pageant Ever" is vital in bringing this uplifting narrative to life. The film, set in a beautiful small-town hamlet over the holiday season, portrays the elegance and simplicity of a tight-knit neighborhood. Jenkins uses cinematography with warm, welcoming tones that inspire nostalgia, resulting in a comfortable ambiance that boosts the festive mood.

The place becomes a character in its own right. The video begins with pictures of a lively town preparing for Christmas—families decorating their homes, children playing in the snow, and neighbors greeting one another with smiles—setting an ideal tone. However, as we meet the Herdmans, we witness their chaotic household—a stunning contrast of clutter and chaos. This visual juxtaposition highlights not just their turbulent past, but also their ultimate change as they interact with the community through the pageant.

Key sequences are brilliantly filmed to accentuate the differences even more. For example, during scenes in the Herdman home, the camera catches their hectic energy—kids running about, loud voices clashing—creating a feeling of disorder that reflects their existence. Church settings, on the other hand, are illuminated with soft, ethereal light that creates a sense of tranquility and reverence. This distinction graphically emphasizes the transition from chaos to harmony.

Natural lighting contributes significantly to the film's emotional passages. During important sequences, particularly those involving the Nativity story, soft focus methods provide an almost dreamy air that imbues them with mystique. The cinematography captures not just pictures but also emotions; each shot is filled with warmth and authenticity, drawing viewers into an intimate but universal experience.

Color has an important role in defining the tone. The warm reds and greens associated with Christmas are predominant throughout church scenes, providing a welcoming ambiance that contrasts dramatically with the colder tones found in the Herdman house. This decision reflects not just their chaotic lifestyle, but also their quest toward acceptance in the community.

Memorable scenes

Several passages in "The Best Christmas Pageant Ever" stand out for their directing and cinematography, creating an indelible effect on viewers. One such scenario takes place during the initial auditions when the Herdmans burst into the chapel. The camera shows their disruptive conduct, juxtaposed with astonished reactions from other youngsters and adults. Jenkins skillfully employs close-up views to show Grace Bradley's anguish as she considers her huge task ahead, while also capturing her tenacity.

Another notable moment occurs during the Herdmans' first rehearsal. The camera follows these brothers as they mumble through their lines and gestures, mispronouncing phrases and fumbling over their cues, resulting in a humorous yet charming montage that highlights their ignorance of the Christmas tale while also emphasizing their desire to learn. This moment is full of laughter, but it also speaks to deeper concepts of acceptance and understanding; despite their flaws, these youngsters are prepared to try something new.

The film's climax—the night of the real pageant—is both visually and emotionally stunning. The chapel is packed with eager residents; you can practically feel their collective breath held in suspense. Jenkins brilliantly creates tension with a blend of broad views that capture the entire scenario and intimate close-ups that focus on people's emotions, notably Grace Bradley's as she sees her vision come to life.

During her performance, Imogene cradles the baby doll representing Jesus, and her tear-filled eyes reveal tremendous vulnerability—a striking visual that captures not just her personal journey but also the film's broader message of redemption and hope. The lighting changes slowly during this scene, becoming softer and more ethereal as if to emphasize Imogene's development from a defiant youngster to someone who exemplifies compassion.

In addition to these critical passages, Jenkins uses smart editing techniques throughout key moments, such as fast cuts between individuals' emotions during rehearsals, to breathe life into otherwise ordinary exchanges. This strategy engages audiences while improving comic timing.

In conclusion, Dallas Jenkins' directing, along with intelligent cinematography, takes *"The Best Christmas Pageant Ever"* from a basic children's narrative to a moving holiday classic that captivates audiences on numerous levels. The painstaking attention to detail in character development, along with seamless mixes of comedy and heart, results in a film that is both enjoyable and profoundly significant.

Jenkins creates an experience that lasts long after viewing, reminding us all that Christmas is about connection, love, and discovering joy in unexpected places. The film urges us to reflect on our own lives while upholding virtues like compassion and understanding—a message that resonates long after the titles roll.

Finally, "The Best Christmas Pageant Ever" demonstrates how creative directing and cinematography can elevate a basic story into a timeless celebration of humanity's ability to love and change during one of our most beloved seasons. Jenkins crafts not only a picture but an experience that challenges us all to embrace compassion at this precious time of year—and beyond.

Fun Facts

- ***Cinematographic Techniques:*** The final pageant scene was shot in a single take to capture the raw emotion of the moment.

- ***Location Scouting:*** The church used in the film was a local historic building, adding authenticity to the setting.

Interactive Quiz

1. Who directed *"The Best Christmas Pageant Ever"*?
 - a) Dallas Jenkins
 - b) Steven Spielberg
 - c) Tim Burton
 - d) Christopher Nolan

2. What visual style does the film predominantly use?
   - a) Dark and moody
   - b) Warm and inviting
   - c) Cold and sterile
   - d) Futuristic and sleek

3. What is a key visual element during the pageant scenes?
   - a) The use of natural lighting
   - b) High-tech special effects
   - c) Black and white imagery
   - d) Animated sequences

Discussion Questions

- Discuss how Dallas Jenkins' direction contributes to the overall tone and message of the film. What directorial choices stand out to you?

- How does the cinematography enhance the storytelling in the movie? Provide examples of key scenes that are visually impactful.

- In what ways do the visual elements of the film help convey the themes of redemption and community?

Chapter 6: Performances

Exclusive Production Notes

- **Casting Process:** The casting team sought actors who could bring both humor and depth to their roles, particularly for the Herdman siblings.

- **Character Chemistry:** The cast spent time together off set to build chemistry, resulting in more authentic interactions on screen.

Outstanding Performances

The cast of "The Best Christmas Pageant Ever" gives outstanding performances, bringing depth and charm to the story. Their performances not only add to the tale but also strike an emotional chord with the audience.

- ***Judy Greer as Grace Bradley:*** Judy Greer delivers a standout performance as Grace Bradley, the hesitant director of the Christmas pageant. Greer's performance is both emotional and realistic, portraying Grace's early anger with the rambunctious Herdmans but also demonstrating her eventual move toward compassion and understanding. Grace is burdened by the work at hand from the start, and Greer portrays this beautifully through subtle facial expressions and body language—her furrowed brow and irritated sighs reveal volumes about her internal struggle.

As the plot develops, Greer enables Grace's

kindness and drive to shine through, giving her a primary, anchoring force in the picture. One especially moving scene happens when Grace defends the Herdmans in front of suspicious community members, demonstrating her tenacious fight for inclusiveness. This scene exemplifies her character's development and devotion to accepting others who are different. Greer's ability to blend comedy and real passion makes Grace an accessible figure for anybody who has experienced obstacles while attempting to do the right thing.

- ***Beatrice Schneider as Imogene Herdman:*** Beatrice Schneider gives an outstanding performance as Imogene Herdman, the eldest and most terrifying of the Herdman siblings. Schneider portrays

Imogene's rough exterior—her rebellious posture and biting tongue—but also reveals her underlying weakness. Imogene's depth makes her a captivating character; her metamorphosis from a rebellious troublemaker to a little girl moved by the Christmas narrative is both dramatic and poignant.

Schneider does an excellent job depicting Imogene's emotional journey. For example, during rehearsals, we witness hints of her insecurity as she struggles with the part of Mary. In one scene, her arrogance wanes as she learns to comprehend Mary's struggles—a moment that Schneider captures with true honesty. Her acting brilliantly captures Imogene's journey from resistance to empathy, urging listeners to see past her flaws and acknowledge her ability for goodness.

- ***Lauren Graham as Mrs. Armstrong:*** Lauren Graham's supporting role as Mrs. Armstrong serves as both comedic relief and a reminder of the community's early opposition to change. Her exaggerated injury—breaking her leg—serves as a trigger for the events that follow, and Graham delivers this with wonderful comedic timing. Her character's interfering actions are both amusing and realistic; she represents the well-intentioned but mistaken adult who fails to adjust to new concepts.

One notable scene is Mrs. Armstrong attempting to lead rehearsals from her wheelchair, resulting in a sequence of humorous blunders that highlight her enthusiastic personality. Graham's portrayal adds dimensions to the story by demonstrating how certain people in the community are resistant to new ideas while others welcome change, which contrasts well with Grace's open-heartedness.

Chemistry between characters

One of the film's finest elements is the connection between the characters, which creates a believable and fascinating dynamic that draws the audience into their world.

- *Grace and Beth Bradley:* The mother-daughter bond between Grace (Judy

Greer) and Beth (Molly Belle Wright) lends emotional depth to the plot. Their interactions are real and emotional, demonstrating the supporting relationship they have. Beth's appreciation for her mother's tenacity grows as she observes Grace overcoming obstacles with resolve.

Wright portrays Beth's young innocence while also depicting moments of insight that show her character development throughout the film. In one moving moment, Beth expresses worry for Imogene after watching her problems during rehearsals, indicating how she internalizes her mother's lessons in compassion. This bond acts as a foundation for both characters; as they confront challenges together, their mutual respect grows, making their journey relevant to anybody who has experienced similar familial dynamics.

- **The Herdman Siblings:** The dynamic between the Herdman siblings, led by Imogene, is chaotic yet adorable, creating a real kinship. Schneider's Imogene leads with tenacity, while Ralph (Jaxon Ashworth), Leroy (played by another talented young actor), Claude (also played by a young actor), Ollie (another sibling), and Gladys (Emma Jacobson) all bring distinct personalities to their family dynamic.

Their rough-and-tumble interactions are depicted with genuineness; times of squabbling are offset with real tenderness, demonstrating their devotion to one another. For example, during a practice scene in which they are unable to recall their lines, their lighthearted taunting displays not only sibling rivalry but also deep-seated love and support inside their chaotic family. This realism makes their ultimate softening and assimilation into the community all the more moving.

- ***Grace Bradley and the Herdmans:*** The film's central theme is Grace Bradley's growing connection with the Herdmans. Grace's patience and understanding eventually win over these wild toddlers, who first fight and misbehave. This process is depicted sensitively; viewers see how Grace's generosity begins to tear down walls.

Grace offers a personal tale about her own

childhood hardships during a rehearsal, which has a strong impact on Imogene. This discussion not only demonstrates Grace's eagerness to connect, but it also functions as a watershed moment for Imogene, who begins to perceive Grace as more than simply an authoritative figure, but as someone who actually cares about her.

Impact of Child Actors

The young actors in "The Best Christmas Pageant Ever" deliver memorable performances that are both realistic and energetic.

- ***Molly Belle Wright as Beth Bradley:*** Wright delivers an appealing and honest performance as both narrator and central protagonist. Her portrayal of Beth's transition from skepticism to adoration for the Herdmans is convincing and sympathetic. Wright conveys Beth's innocence while still communicating flashes of insight that show her development over the novel.

Her emotional acting helps listeners to connect with Beth on a human level, whether she is expressing reservations about involving the Herdmans or applauding their triumphs during rehearsals. Wright adds dimension to every scene she is in. One especially heartbreaking moment happens when Beth defends

Imogene against other students at school—a vital event that demonstrates not just her character growth but also themes of acceptance and understanding.

- ***Jaxon Ashworth's portrayal of Ralph Herdman is rich and nuanced.*** Ashworth blends Ralph's harsh exterior—his swaggering confidence—with unexpected empathy that reveals his character's depth. Ashworth's portrayal of Joseph in the pageant is particularly moving; he depicts Ralph's struggle to retain his tough-guy character while dealing with new obligations.

During critical passages in which he interacts with Imogene or other characters in vulnerable moments—for example, when he hesitates before delivering his lines—Ashworth humanizes Ralph in ways that viewers find genuinely moving. His portrayal allows spectators to see not just a troublemaker, but a young child struggling with his identity amid his turbulent family dynamic.

- **_Emma Jacobson as Gladys Herdman:_** Emma Jacobson shines as Gladys Herdman, the youngest sibling whose energy knows no boundaries. Gladys is infused with contagious energy by Jacobson, whose uncensored honesty contributes to much of the film's humor while also adding an unexpected yet emotional aspect when she plays the Angel of the Lord during the pageant.

Jacobson's depiction captures both innocence and excitement; whether she's yelling lines or engaging with other characters in deliciously uncomfortable ways, Gladys is an indelible presence throughout the film. Her ability to communicate real enthusiasm makes her character sympathetic, reminding viewers of how toddlers frequently approach life without pretense or fear.

The kid actors' performances offer an important depth of genuineness and charm to the picture, making it more accessible to audiences of all ages. Their ability to express true emotions, whether via laughter or sorrow, results in unforgettable moments that last long after viewing.

In summary, "The Best Christmas Pageant Ever" has outstanding performances from the whole group, especially the younger players. The relationship between individuals increases emotional involvement while also adding complexity to each plot. Whether it's Judy Greer's caring leadership or Beatrice Schneider's transforming journey as Imogene, each performance adds something to this uplifting story about acceptance, repentance, and understanding during one of our most beloved seasons.

Finally, these performances transport spectators to a realm where laughter and tears coexist, serving as a reminder that even amid chaos, love can thrive if we allow ourselves to completely embrace it.

Fun Facts

- **Judy Greer's Approach:** To prepare for her role as Grace Bradley, Judy Greer visited community theaters and spoke with local directors to understand the challenges they face.

- **Child Actors:** The young actors portraying the Herdmans had weekly workshops to bond and develop their characters, making their on-screen relationships more believable.

Interactive Quiz

1. Who plays the role of Grace Bradley?
 - a) Lauren Graham
 - b) Judy Greer
 - c) Beatrice Schneider

- d) Molly Belle Wright

2. Which child actor plays Imogene Herdman?
- a) Emma Jacobson
- b) Jaxon Ashworth
- c) Beatrice Schneider
- d) Molly Belle Wright

3. How is the chemistry between the Herdman siblings portrayed?
- a) Distant and cold
- b) Chaotic but endearing
- c) Professional and formal
- d) Structured and disciplined

Discussion Questions

- Analyze Judy Greer's performance as Grace Bradley. How does she bring depth and authenticity to the character?

- Discuss the portrayal of the Herdman siblings. How do the child actors contribute to the film's charm and relatability?

- How do the interactions between the characters enhance the emotional impact of the story? Provide specific examples.

Chapter 7: Comparison with the Book

Exclusive Production Notes

- **Adaptation Choices:** The screenplay closely follows Barbara Robinson's book but introduces new scenes to expand character backstories, making the story richer for the screen.

- **Direct Input:** Dallas Jenkins consulted with Barbara Robinson's family to ensure the film stayed true to the spirit of the book.

Differences and similarities

Adapting a beloved book into a film is always a difficult task, and *"The Best

Christmas Pageant Ever" is no exception. Barbara Robinson's famous children's book has been a beloved holiday read for decades, and adapting it to the screen requires a delicate balance of keeping its charm while making necessary changes for visual storytelling. The adaptation process frequently includes not just translating the material but also reworking it in a way that appeals to both longstanding followers and new audiences.

Similarities:
- **Core Storyline:** The film sticks to the book's central plot, focusing on the Herdmans' daring seizure of the Christmas pageant and the resulting pandemonium, which eventually leads to their metamorphosis. The core of the

characters—each with their own idiosyncrasies and personalities—is carefully retained, ensuring that readers will recognize their favorite moments and interactions. Key storyline aspects, such as the community's first reaction to the Herdmans' antics and the uplifting conclusion that follows, are shown with care, letting viewers see the old story in a new light.

- **Themes:** Both the film and the novel include important themes such as redemption, second chances, and the genuine spirit of Christmas. Both versions emphasize the Herdmans' journey from outcasts to vital members of society. These themes run throughout the story, highlighting the possibility of positive transformation for everyone. The film captures these ideas through moving scenes that match the book's teachings of love, acceptance, and understanding, ensuring that its heart stays intact.

Differences:

- ***Character Development:*** One noticeable distinction is the enhanced character development shown in the film. While Robinson's novel concentrates on the Herdmans and their immediate influence on the pageant, the film delves further into important people's backstories and motives, such as Grace Bradley and her daughter Beth. This increased dimension enriches the story by contextualizing their actions and feelings, allowing viewers to relate more deeply to their experiences.

For example, Grace's challenges as a mother balancing her obligations with her work as a director are portrayed in greater depth. We see her moments of uncertainty and anger, but also her unwavering drive to provide a meaningful experience for everyone participating. Similarly, Beth's character arc is developed; her initial distrust of the Herdmans turns into adoration as she sees them mature.

- **Visual aspects:** As a visual medium, cinema introduces aspects that are not found in the text. The film has rich locations, such as crowded streets decorated for the holidays and hectic yet uplifting sequences during pageant preparations, that add to the story's liveliness. These visual enhancements contribute to an immersive experience that words alone cannot express.

The cinematography amplifies emotional moments by employing lighting and frame to elicit feelings of nostalgia and warmth during critical situations. Scenes representing family gatherings or community celebrations, for example, use warm hues to reflect the heart of the Christmas season. In contrast, scenes set in the Herdman home use colder tones to portray their chaotic lifestyle, visually accentuating their difficulties.

- *pace:* The movie's pace differs from that of the book; several scenes are extended or cut to fit within a cinematic timeframe. Jenkins, for example, spends more screen time establishing the Herdmans' terrible reputation at school before they arrive for auditions. This option helps viewers understand their effect on people around them more thoroughly.

In contrast, some of the book's most thorough explanations have been condensed for a more compact watching experience that retains engagement without compromising clarity. This tempo modification keeps viewers interested in the tale while also ensuring that critical plot aspects are successfully delivered.

Adherence to the Source Material

Overall, *"The Best Christmas Pageant Ever"* is a faithful adaptation of Barbara Robinson's famous book. The filmmakers carefully considered how to bring this beloved story to life on screen, blending authenticity to the source material with cinematic narrative demands. Fans of Robinson's work will notice that, while certain subtleties may alter owing to format limits, the film retains the heart and comedy of the original narrative while also providing new insights through its visual and emotional representation.

The filmmakers' adherence to Robinson's original text is clear in how they preserve crucial exchanges and memorable moments from the novel. Iconic phrases given by characters retain their appeal on film, allowing long standing fans to relive their favorite moments while also exposing new audiences to these renowned statements.

Personal Perspective on the Adaptation

As someone who has read Barbara Robinson's book and seen the film adaptation several times, I find this rendition to be a pleasant success that strikes a deep chord with me. The film captures not just the charm but also the turmoil of the Herdmans' narrative, providing layers of complexity and visual appeal that improve my entire viewing experience.

The performances, particularly those of Judy Greer as Grace Bradley and Beatrice Schneider as Imogene, add additional depth to their characters, making them feel more real and accessible than ever before. Their performances allow listeners to see progress not only via language but also through nuanced emotions and exchanges that wonderfully convey emotion.

The additional character development adds to my comprehension of Grace's motivations as she balances her roles as mother and director, as well as Beth's path from skepticism to appreciation for her mother's fortitude. This deeper examination gives their connection a more natural sense, reflecting real-life tensions between parents and children who must learn from one another.

Furthermore, witnessing Imogene's path play out on television offers a heartbreaking reminder of redemption's eternal appeal—the concept that even people who appear lost may find their way back through love and acceptance. The visual storytelling adds to this message; watching Imogene evolve from a stubborn toddler to someone who epitomizes kindness is quite poignant.

In conclusion, *"The Best Christmas Pageant Ever"* is more than just an adaptation; it exemplifies how tales may change while remaining true to their beginnings. Whether you've read Robinson's book before or are seeing it for the first time on film, it's a wonderful Christmas experience full of fun, love, and crucial lessons about community and kindness—elements that will stay with you long after you've finished watching.

This adaptation offers not just entertainment but also an invitation for contemplation, allowing viewers of all ages to explore how they may embody these principles in their own lives during this season of giving. Finally, whether you read Robinson's original narrative or see the film adaptation, both versions highlight timeless qualities that transcend generations: love, understanding, and hope for redemption in the midst of life's trials.

Fun Facts

- ***Direct Adaptation:*** Many of the film's dialogues are lifted directly from the book, preserving Robinson's original voice.

- ***Audience Reaction:*** Early screenings included fans of the book, who provided feedback that helped shape the final cut.

Interactive Quiz

1. Who is the author of the original book?
   - a) Barbara Robinson
   - b) J.K. Rowling
   - c) Roald Dahl
   - d) Dr. Seuss

2. What is one major similarity between the book and the movie?

   - a) The book and movie have entirely different plots
   - b) Both focus on the Herdmans' involvement in the Christmas pageant
   - c) The book is a mystery, while the movie is a comedy
   - d) The book does not include the character

of Grace Bradley

3. How does the movie expand on the character development compared to the book?

 - a) By adding new characters
 - b) By providing deeper backstories and motivations
 - c) By changing the setting
 - d) By shortening the storyline

Discussion Questions

- Compare the portrayal of the Herdmans in the book and the movie. How do the visual elements of the movie enhance their characterization?
- Discuss how the film's pacing differs from

that of the book. What impact does this have on storytelling?

- Reflect on the faithfulness of the adaptation. Do you think the movie stays true to the spirit of Barbara Robinson's book? Why or why not?

Chapter 8: Audience Reception

Exclusive Production Notes

- **Early Screenings:** Test screenings helped the filmmakers fine-tune the film's pacing and humor, ensuring it resonated with both fans of the book and new audiences.

- **Social Media Campaign:** The marketing team used social media to engage with fans, sharing behind-the-scenes content and interactive polls to build anticipation.

Review and Ratings

"The Best Christmas Pageant Ever" has

received a mixed response from reviewers and spectators alike, demonstrating the film's impact and effectiveness in bringing Barbara Robinson's cherished narrative to life. Critics lauded the picture for its accurate adaptation, emotional depth, and strong performances that spoke to audiences on several levels. The film has a high rating on prominent review aggregator sites, showing universal approbation and admiration from both reviewers and audiences.

Critical Reviews:

- **Variety:** This publication describes the film as "a delightful adaptation that manages to capture the chaotic charm and heartfelt message of the original book." They commend Dallas Jenkins' direction and

Judy Greer's performance as Grace Bradley, noting that "the film strikes a perfect balance between humor and heart." This highlights Jenkins' ability to intertwine laughter with poignant moments, creating an engaging experience for viewers of all ages. The review underlines that the film captures the essence of the novel while also making it more accessible to a modern audience.

- **The Hollywood Reporter:** This site highlights that the film "perfectly balances humor and emotion," describing it as a must-see holiday classic. They enjoy how the Herdmans' transition is both convincing and moving, reminding viewers of the genuine spirit of Christmas. The cinematography and directing are lauded for bringing the narrative to life and conveying the idea of community and redemption. This review emphasizes how the film not only entertains but also conveys profound truths that resonate strongly with its target demographic, making it an important addition to holiday viewing traditions.

- **Rotten Tomatoes:** The film has a good rating on Rotten Tomatoes, with critics praising the accurate adaptation and great performances by its cast. It has an amazing approval rating of 89%, with the opinion being that "the movie is a heartwarming and faithful rendition of a beloved book." This number indicates both critical acclaim and public delight, cementing its place as a Christmas favorite. The high rating suggests that viewers value both the entertainment value and the deeper concepts weaved throughout the story.

Audience Ratings:

Audiences praised the film's vintage appeal, intriguing performers, and meaningful message. Viewer ratings on sites such as IMDb and Rotten Tomatoes indicate the good feedback. The film has an average IMDb rating of 8.5/10, with many viewers having personal connections to the subject. Comments from viewers frequently express thanks for a video that captures the heart of Christmas while entertaining the entire family.

Many viewers have commented that they were transported back to their childhoods when viewing the video. Comments such,

"This movie reminded me of reading the book with my family every Christmas," demonstrate how deeply personal ties may improve enjoyment and appreciation for adaptations.

Audience Reactions

The social media buzz about "The Best Christmas Pageant Ever" has been tremendously positive, with viewers eagerly expressing their opinions and experiences after seeing the video. Hashtags like #BestChristmasPageantEver and #HerdmansRule have trended on Twitter and Instagram, demonstrating the film's broad appeal and influence.

Common Themes in Audience Responses:

- **Nostalgia:** Many viewers have good memories of reading Robinson's book as children and are delighted to see this beloved story brought to life on film. The film's ability to revive these beloved recollections has played a crucial role in its success. Comments like, "I grew up reading this book, and seeing it on screen brought back so many wonderful memories," connect with many others who have had similar experiences. This nostalgia fosters a sense of connection to both the narrative and the common family customs that accompany Christmas storytelling.

- ***Family-Friendly Entertainment:*** The film's wholesome nature appeals to audiences, making it an excellent choice for family viewing over the holiday season. Parents have complimented it for sending positive messages about inclusion and community involvement while also engaging youngsters in talks about what Christmas actually means. One viewer wrote, "Finally, a movie we can all enjoy together without worrying; my kids loved it, and so did we!" This emotion reflects a widespread desire for family-friendly films that stimulate significant talks about values such as kindness and forgiveness.

- ***Emotional Impact:*** Viewers have expressed that the film has brought them to tears, especially at climax parts like the pageant itself. The Herdmans' metamorphosis from outcasts to accepted members of the society strikes a profound chord with spectators, emphasizing themes of redemption and forgiveness. "I never expected to cry this much during a Christmas movie. The Herdmans' story is so touching," observed another observer. These emotional responses demonstrate how well the film communicates its thoughts through relevant narrative.

Social Media Buzz

Fans have used social media to share their favorite scenes, noteworthy phrases, and personal views on "The Best Christmas Pageant Ever." User-generated content, such as fan art, memes, response videos, and even TikTok challenges, has helped boost the film's online visibility and appeal.

Twitter:

- "Just watched #BestChristmasPageantEver and I'm not crying; you are! Such a beautiful film about second chances and the true spirit of Christmas. 🎄🖤" This tweet captures not just individual feeling but also promotes camaraderie among viewers who have similar sentiments.

- "The Herdmans are my new favorite family! Loved every chaotic moment of #BestChristmasPageantEver. A must-watch this holiday season!" This passion demonstrates how fans relate with characters that are both mischievous and kind.

Instagram:

- "Caught the Christmas spirit early with #BestChristmasPageantEver! Loved Judy Greer's performance as Grace Bradley—she truly brought her character to life! ★" These posts showcase individual connections to performances while recognizing favorite actors.

- "Family movie night success! The kids and I couldn't stop laughing and crying. #BestChristmasPageantEver is officially our new holiday tradition! 🎬🎭" This remark shows how films may build enduring family memories via shared experiences.

YouTube:

- **Reaction Videos:** Popular YouTubers' reaction videos have helped to spread the word about the film. Many people praise its combination of humor and poignant moments, making it a top pick for Christmas movie suggestions. One prominent YouTuber wrote, "This movie took me on an emotional rollercoaster! I laughed, I cried, and I loved every second of it." These comments demonstrate how powerful storytelling can be across several platforms.

- ***Reviews and Discussions:*** Video reviews on topics, performances, and overall effect have received thousands of views. These videos frequently go into deeper themes within the film, such as communal acceptance or personal progress, which resonate with people looking for meaningful storylines beyond surface-level enjoyment.

The enthusiastic reaction from both

reviewers and audiences demonstrates the success of *"The Best Christmas Pageant Ever."* The film's ability to relate with viewers of all ages, along with its accurate adaptation of a famous novel, has cemented its place as a new holiday classic. Its success on social media emphasizes its impact by fostering a feeling of community among viewers who share their experiences with this poignant story.

In conclusion, *"The Best Christmas Pageant Ever"* has captivated hearts across generations due to its fascinating storyline, sympathetic characters, emotional depth, and nostalgic appeal. As families gather around screens this holiday season, they discover not just amusement but also important lessons about generosity, acceptance, and redemption—reminders that reverberate long after the credits roll.

This reception not only celebrates individual experiences, but also fosters connections among viewers who appreciate stories that touch on universal themes relevant in today's world—making *"The Best Christmas Pageant Ever"* more than just a holiday film; it becomes an enduring reminder of what it means to be a part of a community united by love and understanding during one of our most cherished seasons.

Fun Facts

- **Positive Feedback:** The film received standing ovations at several early screenings, indicating its strong emotional impact.

- **Celebrity Endorsements:** Several celebrities tweeted their praise for the film, boosting its visibility and appeal.

Interactive Quiz

1. What is the movie's rating on Rotten Tomatoes?
   - a) 50%
   - b) 75%
   - c) 89%
   - d) 95%

2. What hashtag has trended on social media related to the movie?

   - a) #ChristmasPageant
   - b) #BestChristmasPageantEver

- c) #HolidaySpirit
- d) #HerdmanHeroes

3. What common theme do audience reactions highlight?

- a) Dislike for the movie
- b) Nostalgia and emotional impact
- c) Confusion about the plot
- d) Interest in the soundtrack

Discussion Questions

- How has social media influenced the popularity of "The Best Christmas Pageant Ever"? Provide examples of audience reactions.

- Discuss the common themes in critics'

reviews. How do they reflect the strengths and weaknesses of the film?

- What aspects of the film have contributed to its positive reception by audiences? Share your thoughts on the movie's lasting impact.

Chapter 9: Conclusion

Overall Impression

"The Best Christmas Pageant Ever" is a sweet and amusing film that perfectly captures the essence of Barbara Robinson's popular novel. This adaptation brings to life a story that has stayed with readers for decades, combining an interesting storyline, unforgettable characters, and profound truths that speak to the spirit. Director Dallas Jenkins has successfully converted the story into a cinematic experience that is both fun and profound, making it an ideal complement to Christmas traditions.

One of the film's greatest qualities is its

ability to combine comedy with emotion. The Herdman siblings' tumultuous antics generate lots of laughs, highlighting their wild and unpredictable personalities. Their naughty conduct, such as taking food during auditions or disrupting practices, provides funny relief while also emphasizing their challenges and insecurities. However, their final metamorphosis and the community's acceptance of them add poignancy to the narrative. This dichotomy keeps viewers interested, allowing them to experience the entire range of human emotion.

Judy Greer's performance as Grace Bradley is particularly remarkable; she handles the obstacles of managing the pageant with grace, drive, and understanding. Greer reflects Grace's persona as a dedicated mother who is both burdened by her obligations and determined to make a difference in her neighborhood. Her acting captures the spirit of a lady working to bring people together over the holidays, making her accessible to everyone who has encountered similar struggles in their own life.

The young actors' performances bring realism and appeal to the picture, expanding its emotional terrain. Beatrice Schneider excels as Imogene Herdman, conveying her harsh demeanor while showing her underlying tenderness. Schneider's ability to depict Imogene's transformation—from rebellious troublemaker to someone moved by the Christmas spirit—makes her character engaging and relatable. The cast's chemistry heightens the emotional impact of the plot, allowing viewers to empathize with each character's journey on a personal level.

Recommendation for Viewers

"The Best Christmas Pageant Ever" is a must-see for everyone looking for a heartwarming holiday film that authentically portrays the genuine spirit of Christmas. Whether you're a fan of Barbara Robinson's original novel or are discovering this uplifting story for the first time, the film has something for everyone. Families will love the healthy material and encouraging lessons about acceptance, generosity, and community involvement. Viewers of all ages will enjoy the comedy and emotional moments that elicit both laughter and introspection.

The film's themes of redemption, second chances, and the actual spirit of Christmas are especially relevant during this season, making it an excellent addition to any holiday movie schedule. It inspires viewers to think on their own lives and relationships, reminding us all that love and compassion may result in great transformations in ourselves and those around us.

For those who like stories about community links, family connections, and the power of compassion, *"The Best Christmas Pageant Ever"* is guaranteed to become a family favourite. Its ageless appeal and important lessons make it a video that can be watched year after year, acting as a reminder of compassion and understanding during one of our most precious moments.

Final Thoughts

As we ponder on "The Best Christmas Pageant Ever," it is evident that this film has accomplished something genuinely remarkable. By remaining loyal to the spirit of Barbara Robinson's novel while adding additional levels of depth and visual appeal, it has won the hearts of both viewers and reviewers. Its popularity demonstrates the lasting power of narrative and universal themes that appeal to audiences across generations.

To summarize, *"The Best Christmas Pageant Ever"* is more than a holiday picture; it is a celebration of the human spirit. It serves as a reminder that everyone, regardless of background or previous misdeeds, has the capacity for personal growth and repentance. The Herdman siblings' journey—who begin as misfits but eventually find acceptance—and encounters with Grace Bradley and her community remind us of what Christmas actually means: love, acceptance, forgiveness, and understanding.

As you watch this film with your loved ones this Christmas season, may you be inspired by its profound themes while also finding delight in its humor and heartwarming scenes. *"The Best Christmas Pageant Ever"* is more than simply a narrative; it's a memorable experience that stays with you long after the credits roll. It gives you a renewed feeling of optimism and a greater appreciation for the enchantment that this time of year delivers.

This short asks us all to open our hearts during this holiday season—to accept those who are different from us—and to understand that everyone has something unique to offer. In doing so, we not only enhance our own lives, but also foster communities of love and acceptance—an important message that will reverberate long after the holiday season is over.

Finally, *"The Best Christmas Pageant Ever"* serves as a timeless reminder that there is always a place for compassion and understanding in the midst of life's turbulence, whether it's familial conflicts or social divides. As we gather around screens with family and friends each December, let us carry on the lessons learnt from Grace Bradley and her odd companions—the Herdmans—who educate us about embracing our shared humanity during one of our most beloved seasons.

As you ponder on this narrative in your own life, may it motivate you to look for chances for kindness in your daily interactions. Allow *"The Best Christmas Pageant Ever"* to not only entertain, but also act as a catalyst for change in how we see one another, reminding us all that love can convert even the most chaotic conditions into something beautiful during this lovely time of year.

Interactive Quiz

1. What is the primary message of *"The Best Christmas Pageant Ever"*?
   - a) The importance of wealth
   - b) The power of community, love, and redemption
   - c) The value of competition
   - d) The joy of material gifts

2. Who is the most influential character in changing the Herdmans' behavior?
   - a) Mrs. Armstrong
   - b) Grace Bradley
   - c) Beth Bradley
   - d) Ralph Herdman

3. What significant event marks the turning point in the Herdmans' understanding of

Christmas?

- a) The first rehearsal
- b) The day of the pageant
- c) Learning about the birth of Jesus
- d) Their initial arrival at the church

Discussion Questions

- Reflect on the primary message of *"The Best Christmas Pageant Ever."* How does the movie convey this message through its characters and plot?

- Discuss the impact of the movie on viewers' perceptions of the Christmas season. How does it enhance or change traditional views of the holiday?

- What makes *"The Best Christmas Pageant Ever"* a timeless holiday classic? How does it compare to other holiday films you've seen?

- How does the transformation of the Herdmans influence the community's understanding of acceptance and forgiveness? Provide examples from the film.

Chapter 10: Additional Resources

Exclusive Production Notes

- **Digital Extras:** The film's digital release includes bonus features such as director's commentary, deleted scenes, and a making-of documentary.

- **Educational Content:** The production team created educational materials for schools and community groups, emphasizing the film's themes of redemption and community.

Where to Watch the Movie?

To truly immerse yourself in the wonder of *"The Best Christmas Pageant Ever,"* you may watch this lovely film on many platforms:

- *In theatres:* Those who value the cinematic experience can watch the film in select cinemas. Seeing the film on the large screen helps you to take in the colorful images and sound, which heightens the emotional impact of critical moments. Check your local listings for showtimes, and consider attending with family or friends to experience the fun and joy. The collective environment of a theater may emphasize the film's joyful moments, making it an unforgettable experience.

- **Streaming Services:** If you want to watch from the comfort of your own home, *"The Best Christmas Pageant Ever"* is available on major streaming platforms including Netflix, Amazon Prime Video, and Disney+. Simply search for the film on your preferred provider and spend a relaxing movie night with family or friends. Streaming allows you to pause for snacks or take breaks, giving it a more casual way to watch this holiday favorite.

- **Digital Buy or Rent:** Those interested in owning or renting a digital copy of this charming film may do so through outlets such as iTunes, Google Play, Vudu, and YouTube Movies. Owning a digital copy allows you to relive this beloved narrative whenever you want—ideal for those chilly winter nights when you want to wrap up with a soothing movie.

- **DVD or Blu-ray:** If you prefer tangible copies, the movie is available on DVD and Blu-ray from major shops such as Walmart, Target, and Amazon. Owning a hard copy allows you to view it whenever you want without the need for an online connection, as well as put it in your holiday movie collection for years to come.

Interviews With the Cast and Crew

To learn more about the creation of *"The Best Christmas Pageant Ever,"* check out exclusive interviews with the actors and crew. These discussions offer a behind-the-scenes glimpse at the creative process, production problems, and notable incidents that influenced the film.

- **_Dallas Jenkins, Director:_** Jenkins discusses his plans to adapt this renowned novel into a film in several interviews. He outlines how he balanced faithfulness to Robinson's original plot with the desire to make it visually appealing to current viewers. Jenkins comments on his experiences working with a superb cast and crew, and he hopes that the picture brings audiences joy and purpose.

- **_Judy Greer (Grace Bradley):_** Greer shares insights on her approach to playing Grace Bradley. She reveals how she used her own mothering experiences to give her character emotional depth. Greer reveals her favorite scenes from the filming, particularly those that show Grace's development as she comes to accept the Herdmans despite their chaotic character.

- ***Beatrice Schneider (Imogene Herdman):*** Schneider comments on her role as Imogene, explaining how she related with the character's hardships and eventual change. She tells stories about working with her fellow cast members and how their friendship helped to capture the crazy yet loving dynamic of the Herdman family.

Lauren Graham (Mrs. Armstrong): Graham discusses her part as Mrs. Armstrong and how she addressed bringing comedy into the character. She highlights the film's themes of community and inclusiveness, as well as her experience working with such a large ensemble cast. Her views provide light on how joint efforts influenced the finished result.

These interviews may be found on entertainment news websites, film discussion podcasts, and YouTube channels that specialize in behind-the-scenes movie footage.

Related Articles and Reviews

For those who want to learn more about *"The Best Christmas Pageant Ever,"* there are several articles and reviews that go into various parts of the film. These pieces include critical evaluations, audience reactions, and in-depth explorations of the topics, performances, and overall influence.

- **_Weekly Entertainment:_** An essay showcasing strong performances in the film and analyzing its accurate adaptation of Robinson's novel. The review highlights how wonderfully each character is brought to life on screen, giving readers insight into what makes this adaptation unique.

The New York Times: A comprehensive review that delves into how the film's themes of forgiveness and community resonate with modern audiences. It examines how these ideas are presented via both humorous and heartbreaking moments, giving readers a better understanding of why this narrative is still important today.

- **Film Threat:** This article covers the difficulties of adapting a beloved children's book while also discussing creative decisions made by filmmakers that improve storytelling without losing sight of what made the original work unique. This analysis gives background for readers who want to better understand adaptation processes.

Parent Magazine: An intelligent essay promoting the film as a great family Christmas movie. It promotes good lessons about compassion and inclusion, as well as fascinating material for youngsters. This tip is especially useful for parents looking for healthful watching alternatives throughout the Christmas season.

These pieces are available on their respective websites or are often shared on social media platforms, making them easily accessible to fans wanting to learn more about this heartwarming adoption.

Community Engagement

The influence of *"The Best Christmas Pageant Ever"* goes beyond viewing; it encourages fan interaction and conversations. Consider joining online forums or social media groups where fans may discuss their opinions, experiences, and even fan-created content such as artwork or memes about the film. Platforms like Reddit, Facebook groups dedicated to

Christmas films, and particular movie fan sites are excellent locations to interact with other viewers who share your enthusiasm for this lovely narrative.

Engaging in these forums allows fans to share their thoughts on their favorite scenes from the film or compare them to their recollections of reading Robinson's book. Many fans start discussion threads where they examine character arcs or offer personal tales about issues shown in the film, resulting in a rich tapestry of shared experiences that increases everyone's love for this Christmas classic.

Viewers may improve their knowledge and appreciation of **"The Best Christmas Pageant Ever."** by exploring these supplementary resources, whether through interviews that provide insider viewpoints or articles that offer deeper analysis. These resources add vital context to your viewing experience, making it more pleasurable and memorable.

Whether you're revisiting this classic tale or finding it for the first time, these tools will help you connect with its timeless values of compassion, community spirit, and redemption during one of our most beloved seasons. As you interact with these resources, may they encourage you not only during the holidays but also in your daily life, reminding us all of our ability for kindness and understanding in an ever-changing world.

Fun Facts

-**Director's Commentary:** Dallas Jenkins provides insights into the filmmaking process and the challenges of adapting a beloved book.

- **Deleted Scenes:** Some humorous scenes that didn't make the final cut are included in the bonus features.

Interactive Quiz

1. On which streaming platform can you watch *"The Best Christmas Pageant Ever"*?
 - a) Hulu
 - b) Amazon Prime Video
 - c) HBO Max
 - d) Netflix

2. Who directed *"The Best Christmas Pageant Ever"*?
   - a) Steven Spielberg
   - b) Dallas Jenkins
   - c) Greta Gerwig
   - d) Martin Scorsese

3. What type of content can you find in the book's additional resources section?
   - a) Behind-the-scenes interviews
   - b) Fan fiction stories
   - c) Cooking recipes
   - d) Exercise routines

Discussion Questions

- How do the interviews with the cast and crew enhance your understanding of the film? What new insights did you gain?

- Reflect on the value of interactive quizzes and discussion questions in engaging with the movie. How do they deepen your appreciation for the film?

- Discuss the role of additional resources, such as articles and reviews, in shaping your perception of the movie. How do they contribute to a more comprehensive understanding?

ABOUT THE AUTHOR

Stacey J. Tengan has always been fascinated by the power of storytelling, especially on the big screen. As a movie review writer, she balances her enthusiasm for films with a clever, down-to-earth style that readers enjoy. Stacey's reviews offer more than simply critique; they move into the heart of each picture, delivering insights that are both accessible and interesting.

In her newest book, Stacey takes readers on an intriguing voyage through the highly anticipated **"The Best Christmas Pageant Ever Movie**

Review" movie of 2024. This in-depth guide is filled with unique production notes, fun facts, interactive quizzes, polls, and thought-provoking discussion questions, delivering a full and entertaining overview of the film. Perfect for movie aficionados, trivia lovers, and discussion groups, this guide will take you through the production of the film and beyond.

Stacey's work spans all genres, from tiny independent films to Hollywood blockbusters, helping people uncover new favorites. Whether you're a casual viewer or a film lover, Stacey's reviews are a must-read for anyone looking to look deeper into the world of cinema. Plus, with exclusive previews of forthcoming reviews and material, Stacey ensures that readers are constantly in the loop with the latest in the world of cinema.

Exclusive Christmas Preview

This holiday season brings a collection of must-watch movies that promise to entertain, inspire, and captivate audiences. From festive comedies to thought-provoking dramas, there's something for everyone to enjoy during the most wonderful time of the year.

Red One

Dwayne Johnson and Chris Evans team up in *Red One*, a festive action-comedy that takes viewers on a high-stakes mission to rescue Santa Claus after his mysterious kidnapping from the North

Pole. Packed with humor, heart, and adrenaline-fueled action, this $250 million blockbuster sets out to establish a new Christmas movie franchise. Currently showing in cinemas, *Red One* is a thrilling ride that will soon be available for streaming on Amazon Prime Video.

Meet Me Next Christmas

For those seeking romance and holiday cheer, *Meet Me Next Christmas* offers the perfect blend. Christina Milian stars as Layla, a woman navigating New York City in a desperate yet charming quest to find love and snag tickets to a sold-out Christmas concert. Streaming now on Netflix, this heartwarming romantic comedy captures the magic and excitement of the holiday season, making it an ideal choice for cozy nights in.

Inside Out 2

Pixar's *Inside Out 2* revisits Riley's mind, now as a teenager grappling with new emotions like Anxiety and Envy. The film dives deep into the challenges of growing up, presenting themes of self-discovery and emotional growth. With stunning animation and a heartfelt storyline, this sequel appeals to both kids and adults. While some critics feel it doesn't surpass the original, it remains a moving exploration of adolescence that resonates across generations.

Wicked (2024)

Wicked (2024) brings the iconic Broadway musical to life, delving into the untold backstory of Elphaba and Glinda from *The Wizard of Oz*. Starring Ariana Grande and Cynthia Erivo, this visually stunning adaptation enchants with its lavish design and memorable performances. While some musical numbers have sparked mixed reviews, the film's magical elements and powerful acting make it a standout for fans of musicals and fantasy alike.

Gladiator

The timeless epic *Gladiator* remains a holiday favorite for those seeking dramatic storytelling and action-packed sequences. The tale of Maximus Decimus Meridius, a Roman general seeking vengeance, resonates with themes of loyalty, justice, and honor. Its masterful performances and unforgettable battle scenes make it a classic worth rewatching, especially during the festive season.

The Substance

For viewers who enjoy thought-provoking narratives, *The Substance* provides an intense exploration of the ethical dilemmas faced by scientists. This gripping drama examines the consequences of scientific advancements and challenges audiences to reflect on responsibility and morality. Its deep storytelling and philosophical undertones make it a compelling choice for those seeking meaningful cinema during the holidays.

Whether you're in the mood for heart-pounding action, magical adventures, or reflective dramas, this Christmas lineup offers a diverse array of cinematic delights to brighten your festive season.